Golden Retriever Dog Diary

A dog diary with plenty of space for notes and photos

*The bond with a true dog is as lasting as the
ties of this earth will ever be.
~Konrad Lorenz*

A diary to document your dog's life as it happens!

Dogs are earthly miracles with wagging tails, hearts full of love and the pitter-patter of paws.

Copyright © 2014
By Debbie Miller

This book is © copyrighted by the author, Debbie Miller and is protected under the US Copyright Act of 1976 and all other applicable international, federal, state and local laws, with ALL rights reserved.

This book contains protected material. No part of this may be copied, or changed in any format, sold, or used in any way. Any unauthorized reprint or use of this material is prohibited, including photocopying, recording, or by any information storage and retrieval system without written permission from the author or publisher.

Introduction

A diary for your Golden Retriever to keep your treasured memories and preserve the cherished moments!

There is space for snapshots of your companion! This blank diary gives dog lovers a place to chart their puppy's growth.

As your dog grows into an adult you can document and capture the special moments.

There is a page for birth information, vaccine records, and even a page to place your dog's paw prints!

You can take photos of your puppy discovering his world as he grows into an adult.

Pictures are worth a thousand words, it helps us remember the little moments that bring us such joy in an instant.

Don't miss the special times when your companion is sleeping, bounding across the yard, his first birthday or favorite things to do!

With this dog diary you will be able to admire and preserve your favorite memories to enjoy the precious moments for years!

Start creating a lasting memoir today of your dog!

Yesterday I was a dog. Today I'm a dog. Tomorrow I'll probably still be a dog. Sigh! There's so little hope for advancement.
~Charles M. Schulz

My little dog - a heartbeat at my feet.
~Edith Wharton

*Money will buy a pretty good dog,
but it won't buy the wag of his tail.*
~Josh Billings

"Dogs are not our whole life, but they make our lives whole."
~Roger Caras

The Homecoming

Date your dog joined the family: _____

First Photo

Date of Birth: _____

Place of Birth: _____

Registered Name: _____

Call Name: _____

Father's Name: _____

Mother's Name: _____

Age	Lbs	Oz
6 Weeks		
8 Weeks		
10 Weeks		
3 Months		
4 Months		
6 Months		
8 Months		
10 Months		
1 Year		
2 Years		

Puppy Paw Print

Adult Paw Print

Vaccination Records

Age	Shot Date	Distemper	Parvo	Rabies	Deworm
6 weeks					
10 weeks					
14 weeks					
1 Year					
2 Years					
3 Years					
4 Years					
5 Years					
6 Years					
7 Years					
8 Years					
9 Years					
10 Years					
11 Years					
12 Years					

Heartworm Testing:

1 Year____ 2 Year____ 3 Year ____ 4 Year____ 5 Year____

6 Year____ 7 Year____ 8 Year ____ 9 Year____ 10 Year____

Vaccination Notes:

_____

_____

Medical Record Notes:

Medical Treatments:

Neutered	Spayed	Other

Medical Conditions:

Date	Accidents or Injuries

Medical Emergencies:

Memories

Don't miss the happy moments!

Start creating lasting memories today!

Photo Here

Memories:

Photo Here

Memories:

Photo Here

Memories:

Photo Here

Memories:

Photo Here

Memories:

Photo Here

Memories:

Photo Here

Memories:

Photo Here

Memories:

Photo Here

Memories:

Photo Here

Memories:

Photo Here

Memories:

Photo Here

Memories:

Photo Here

Memories:

Photo Here

Memories

Photo Here

Memories:

Photo Here

Memories:

Photo Here

Memories:

Photo Here

Memories:

Photo Here

Memories:

Photo Here

Memories:

_____

_____

_____

_____

_____

_____

_____

Photo Here

Memories:

Photo Here

Memories:

Photo Here

Memories:

Photo Here

Memories:

Photo Here

Memories:

Photo Here

Memories:

_____

_____

_____

_____

_____

_____

_____

Photo Here

Memories:

Photo Here

Memories:

_____

_____

_____

_____

_____

_____

_____

Photo Here

Memories:

Photo Here

Memories:

Photo Here

Memories:

Photo Here

Memorics:

Photo Here

Memories:

Photo Here

Memories:

Photo Here

Memories:

Photo Here

Memories:

Photo Here

Memories:

Photo Here

Memories:

Photo Here

Memories:

Photo Here

Memories:

_____

_____

_____

_____

_____

_____

_____

Photo Here

Memories:

Photo Here

Memories:

Photo Here

Memories:

Photo Here

Memories:

Photo Here

Memories:

Photo Here

Memories:

Photo Here

Memories:

Photo Here

Memories:

Photo Here

Memories:

Photo Here

Memories:

Photo Here

Memories:

Photo Here

Memories:

Photo Here

Memories:

Photo Here

Memories:

_____

_____

_____

_____

_____

_____

_____

Photo Here

Memories:

Photo Here

Memories:
_____

_____

_____

_____

_____

_____

_____